MAKING THE GRADE

1

EASY POPULAR PIECES FOR YOUNG FLAUTISTS. SELECTED AND ARRA

	PIANO SCORE	FLUTE PART
Any Dream Will Do	3	3
The Skater's Waltz	4	3
Eensy, Weensy Spider	5	4
Pavane (Warlock)	6	4
I'm Popeye The Sailor Man	7	5
Edelweiss	8	5
O No, John!	10	6
Sarabande (Handel)	11	6
I Have A Dream	12	7
The Yellow Rose Of Texas	14	8
Jean de Florette (Theme)	15	8
No Matter What	16	9
Hey Hey Are You Ready To Play (Tweenies Theme)	18	10
Guantanamera	20	10
Barbie Girl	22	11
The Phantom Of The Opera	23	12
Land Of Hope And Glory	24	12
All My Loving	26	13
Somethin' Stupid	28	14
Oom Pah Pah	30	14
Dance To Your Daddy	32	15

Published by
Chester Music
8/9 Frith Street, London W1D 3JB, England.

Exclusive Distributors:
Music Sales Limited
Distribution Centre, Newmarket Road, Bury St. Edmunds, Suffolk IP33 3YB, England.
Music Sales Pty Limited
120 Rothschild Avenue, Rosebery, NSW 2018, Australia.

This book © Copyright 2003 by Chester Music.
Unauthorised reproduction of any part of this publication by any means
including photocopying is an infringement of copyright.

Music arranged and processed by Jerry Lanning.
Edited by Heather Ramage.
Printed in the United Kingdom by Caligraving Limited, Thetford, Norfolk.

CD recorded, mixed and mastered by Jonas Persson.
Flute by John Whelan

www.musicsales.com

This publication is not authorised for sale in the
United States of America and/or Canada.

Chester Music
part of The Music Sales Group
London/New York/Paris/Sydney/Copenhagen/Berlin/Madrid/Tokyo

INTRODUCTION

This collection of 21 popular tunes has been carefully arranged and graded to provide attractive teaching repertoire for young flautists. The familiarity of the material will stimulate pupils' enthusiasm and encourage their practice.

The technical demands of the solo part increase progressively up to the standard of Associated Board Grade 1. The piano accompaniments are simple yet effective and should be within the range of most pianists.

Breath marks are given throughout, showing the most musically desirable places to take a breath.

ANY DREAM WILL DO

(from "Joseph and the Amazing Technicolor® Dreamcoat")

Music by Andrew Lloyd Webber. Lyrics by Tim Rice

Take care with the dotted rhythms. Keep the semiquavers light and try to match the accompaniment.

© Copyright 1969 The Really Useful Group Limited.
All Rights Reserved. International Copyright Secured.

THE SKATER'S WALTZ

By Emil Waldteufel

Try to play the last eight bars in a single breath.

© Copyright 2003 Chester Music Limited, 8/9 Frith Street, London W1D 3JB.
All Rights Reserved. International Copyright Secured.

EENSY, WEENSY SPIDER

American traditional

You'll need to snatch a quick breath in bar 16. Don't be late on the second beat!

PAVANE
(from "The Capriol Suite")
By Peter Warlock

Try for a smooth, sustained sound, but be sure to tongue each note quite firmly.

© Copyright 1928 by Peter Warlock.
This arrangement © Copyright 2003 by Peter Warlock.
Exclusively licensed to and reproduced by kind permission of J Curwen & Sons Limited.
All Rights Reserved.

I'M POPEYE THE SAILOR MAN

Words & Music by Sammy Lerner

This piece needs a bright and breezy performance!

© Copyright 1934 Famous Music Corporation, USA.
All Rights Reserved. International Copyright Secured.

EDELWEISS
(from "The Sound of Music")

Words by Oscar Hammerstein II. Music by Richard Rodgers

Play each phrase as smoothly as possible. Listen carefully to the tuning.

© Copyright 1959 & 1975 Richard Rodgers & The Estate of Oscar Hammerstein II. Williamson Music Company.
All Rights Reserved. International Copyright Secured.

O NO, JOHN!

English traditional

Play the last four bars quite forcefully, for contrast.

© Copyright 2003 Chester Music Limited, 8/9 Frith Street, London W1D 3JB.
All Rights Reserved. International Copyright Secured.

SARABANDE

(from "Keyboard Suite IX")

By George Frideric Handel

In this piece it's probably best to breathe every two bars.

© Copyright 2003 Chester Music Limited, 8/9 Frith Street, London W1D 3JB.
All Rights Reserved. International Copyright Secured.

I HAVE A DREAM

Words & Music by Benny Andersson & Björn Ulvaeus

Make sure you always take a full breath, even though most of the phrases are short.

© Copyright 1979 Union Songs AB, Stockholm, Sweden for the world.
Bocu Music Limited for Great Britain and the Republic of Ireland.
All Rights Reserved. International Copyright Secured.

THE YELLOW ROSE OF TEXAS

American traditional

Play with a full sound, and make sure you tongue each note.

JEAN DE FLORETTE (THEME)

By Jean-Claude Petit

Take your breaths quickly, so that you don't have to cut the dotted minims too short.

© Copyright 1986 Renn Productions SARL, France/SDRM.
All Rights Reserved. International Copyright Secured.

NO MATTER WHAT

Music by Andrew Lloyd Webber. Words by Jim Steinman

Take care with the start of each phrase. It's very easy to be late!

© Copyright 1998 The Really Useful Group Limited (50%)/Lost Boys Music/Universal Music Publishing Limited (50%).
All Rights Reserved. International Copyright Secured.

HEY HEY ARE YOU READY TO PLAY
(Tweenies Theme)

Music by Graham Pike & Liz Kitchen. Words by Will Brenton & Ian Lauchlan

Listen hard to the tuning of the octave leaps. Keep the rhythm relaxed.

© Copyright 2000 BBC Worldwide Music Limited. Administered by BMG Music Publishing Limited.
All Rights Reserved. International Copyright Secured.

GUANTANAMERA

Music adaptation by Pete Seeger & Julian Orbon. Words adapted by Julian Orbon from a poem by José Marti

Keep the rhythm very steady. When a phrase ends with a quaver, play the quaver lightly.

© Copyright 1963 & 1965 Fall River Music Incorporated, USA. Harmony Music Limited.
All Rights Reserved. International Copyright Secured.

BARBIE GIRL

*Words & Music by Soren Rasted, Claus Norreen, Rene Dif,
Lene Nystrom, Johnny Pederson & Karsten Delgado*

Take a good breath on the first beat of bar 6, to carry you through to the end of the phrase.

© Copyright 1997 MCA Music, Scandinavia AB/Warner Chappell Music, Denmark.
Universal/MCA Music Limited (91.67%)/Warner Chappell Music Limited (8.33%).
All Rights Reserved. International Copyright Secured.

THE PHANTOM OF THE OPERA

(from "The Phantom of the Opera")

Music by Andrew Lloyd Webber. Lyrics by Charles Hart. Additional Lyrics by Richard Stilgoe & Mike Batt.

Be absolutely precise with the dotted crotchet/quaver rhythms.

© Copyright 1986 & 1995 The Really Useful Group Limited.
This arrangement © Copyright 2003 The Really Useful Group Limited.
All Rights Reserved. International Copyright Secured.

LAND OF HOPE AND GLORY

By Edward Elgar

Try for a very smooth, sustained sound. Don't let the tempo drag.

© Copyright 1902 by Boosey & Co Ltd.
This arrangement by permission of Boosey & Hawkes Music Publishers Ltd.
All Rights Reserved. International Copyright Secured.

ALL MY LOVING

Words & Music by John Lennon & Paul McCartney

Be careful to read the rhythms carefully – don't guess!

SOMETHIN' STUPID

Words & Music by C. Carson Parks

Articulate the repeated quavers neatly and evenly.

© Copyright 1967 Greenwood Music Company, USA. Montclare Music Company Limited.
All Rights Reserved. International Copyright Secured.

OOM PAH PAH

(from "Oliver")

Words & Music by Lionel Bart

This piece needs a strong performance, but the middle section should be softer and smoother for contrast.

DANCE TO YOUR DADDY

English traditional

Accent the first beat of each bar slightly, but play the other notes quite lightly.

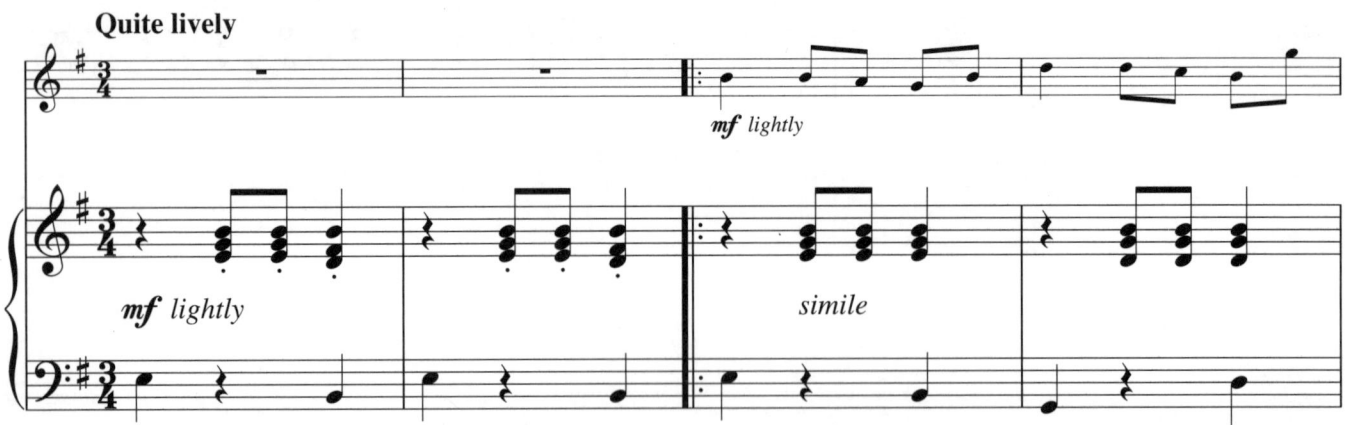

© Copyright 2003 Chester Music Limited, 8/9 Frith Street, London W1D 3JB.
All Rights Reserved. International Copyright Secured.